Everything in Petunia's life was perfect.

Her petals were

POSITIVELY RADIANT

Her schoolwork was

precise

and

praiseworthy,

always earning her a gold star.

She always got to play the particular game
she wanted at recess with her friends.

That was the way
Petunia liked it.

Every day, it was important to Petunia
that she did her very best work in school.

Petunia's paintings
always went
according to plan.

Mr. Zin, the art teacher,
often complimented
Petunia, filling her
with pride.

She practiced her handwriting each day to make sure it was neat, redoing it many times until it was *exactly* the way she imagined.

Petunia *loved* being perfect
and made sure
each day was flawless.

unt

One day Petunia woke up and could not seem to get her petals to sit perfectly.

No matter how hard she tried, she could not get them to look *just right*.

Petunia left for school that day with a little less pep in her step and felt herself *d r o o p.*

The next day wasn't perfect either.

Petunia got the last question on the math test wrong, even though she spent all week

prepping and practicing her math facts.

She slumped lower in her chair
for the rest of the day.

The day *after* that,
Petunia was out at recess
and she wanted to play tag,
but all her friends wanted to play
basketball instead.

Petunia got so frustrated that she
stomped away and sat alone
for the rest of recess, wilted.

When Petunia got back to her classroom, Miss Lily noticed Petunia's unusually dampened mood.

"Petunia, I noticed you're a bit sad today. What's wrong?"

"I haven't been perfect this week," Petunia sorrowfully explained as her head hung low.

"First it was my petals, then it was the mistake on my math test, and today at recess we didn't play the game *I* wanted to..."

Miss Lily brought Petunia in for a hug.
"I know how much you like things
to be a certain way, and
I admire your hard work in school.

But just because we make a mistake,
that doesn't mean we should let it
take our joy away."

“It can be hard when things in our life don't go the way we planned, but that doesn’t mean you are any less

smart,
AMBITIOUS,
beautiful,
or KIND.

Everybody makes mistakes or has unexpected moments and that’s how we learn and grow!”

"I have an idea of how we can help you," Miss Lily said.

"First, I want you to remember that everyone makes mistakes! Remember last week when I accidentally spelt Wednesday wrong when writing our morning message?

It was a quick fix and now I'll never forget how to spell it! I definitely didn't let it stop me from having a great day.

"Then, whenever you are feeling frustrated or nervous
that something is not going perfectly in the classroom,

I want you to take a quick break in our calming corner.
Take some deep breaths, use our tools, and
come back to the activity when you feel more at ease."

And if you can't move your body to a new space,
take some deep breaths where you are
and remind yourself of these affirmations:

I am
trying my best
I know mistakes
help me learn
I can
do hard things
I am loved
for being me

"Mom! Dad!" Petunia called as she rushed into the kitchen after school. "Guess what I'm working on at school?"

“Miss Lily is teaching me some mindfulness strategies
to use when I am feeling
overwhelmed or frustrated.

But it still is really hard
to not get upset
when I make a mistake...”

Petunia’s parents came over to her. “We don't want
Petunia’s dad agreed: “Even if that means your
or are feeling

perfection, Petunia - we want you." said Petunia's mom.

petals are out of sorts, you get a math question wrong, sad.

After that,

Petunia worked hard to be ok with making mistakes, using Miss Lily's ideas whenever she felt upset.

She learned that she could love life and herself even if it—and she—wasn't perfect.

And *that* was how she liked it!

Made in United States
North Haven, CT
09 December 2024